Cambridge Plain Texts

CARLYLE

THE PRESENT TIME

T0346134

CARLYLE

THE PRESENT TIME

CAMBRIDGE
AT THE UNIVERSITY PRESS
1921

CAMBRIDGE UNIVERSITY PRESS
Cambridge, New York, Melbourne, Madrid, Cape Town,
Singapore, São Paulo, Delhi, Mexico City

Cambridge University Press
The Edinburgh Building, Cambridge CB2 8RU, UK

Published in the United States of America by Cambridge University Press, New York

www.cambridge.org
Information on this title: www.cambridge.org/9781107692312

First published 1921
Re-issued 2013

A catalogue record for this publication is available from the British Library

ISBN 978-1-107-69231-2 Paperback

NOTE

THOMAS CARLYLE (1795–1881) once described himself as a "Radical absolutist," and throughout his political essays the chief object of his attack is the Utilitarian school—the school which sought to achieve "the greatest happiness of the greatest number" by recognizing the motive power of enlightened self-interest, the importance of *laissez-faire*, and the efficacy of the parliamentary vote.

To this Carlyle replied, first, that the best in man is not governed by material considerations of pleasure and pain, or of profit and loss; secondly, that *laissez-faire* was the negation of government; and, lastly, that the vote was but a twenty-thousandth share in the National Palaver.

What Society needed was a man with the strength to govern and the integrity to govern well—a hero.

Carlyle's distrust of democracy is evident even in his earlier political writings, but by 1850, when he wrote a series of *Latter-Day Pamphlets*, of which *The Present Time* was the first, his distrust had grown to alarm. He looked at the continent of Europe and saw revolution everywhere; nearer home were the problems of Ireland and of the Chartist movement. The ship of state seemed to him to be sinking; the only hope was to bring the "Captainless under due captaincy."

The Present Time should not be without interest in the year 1921.

S. C. ROBERTS

December 1920

THE PRESENT TIME

THE Present Time, youngest-born of Eternity, child
and heir of all the Past Times with their good and
evil, and parent of all the Future, is ever a 'New Era'
to the thinking man; and comes with new questions
and significance, however commonplace it look: to
know *it*, and what it bids us do, is ever the sum of
knowledge for all of us. This new Day, sent us out of
Heaven, this also has its heavenly omens;—amid the
bustling trivialities and loud empty noises, its silent
monitions, which if we cannot read and obey, it will
not be well with us! No;—nor is there any sin more
fearfully avenged on men and Nations than that same,
which indeed includes and presupposes all manner of
sins: the sin which our old pious fathers called 'judicial blindness;'—which we, with our light habits, may
still call misinterpretation of the Time that now is;
disloyalty to its real meanings and monitions, stupid
disregard of these, stupid adherence active or passive
to the counterfeits and mere current semblances of
these. This is true of all times and days.

But in the days that are now passing over us, even
fools are arrested to ask the meaning of them; few of
the generations of men have seen more impressive
days. Days of endless calamity, disruption, disloca-
tion, confusion worse confounded: if they are not
days of endless hope too, then they are days of utter
despair. For it is not a small hope that will suffice,

the ruin being clearly, either in action or in prospect, universal. There must be a new world, if there is to be any world at all! That human things in our Europe can ever return to the old sorry routine, and proceed with any steadiness or continuance there; this small hope is not now a tenable one. These days of universal death must be days of universal newbirth, if the ruin is not to be total and final! It is a Time to make the dullest man consider; and ask himself, Whence *he* came? Whither he is bound?—A veritable 'New Era,' to the foolish as well as to the wise.

Not long ago the world saw, with thoughtless joy, which might have been very thoughtful joy, a real miracle not heretofore considered possible or conceivable in the world: a Reforming Pope. A simple pious creature, a good country priest, invested unexpectedly with the tiara, takes up the New Testament, declares that this henceforth shall be his rule of governing. No more finesse, chicanery, hypocrisy, or false or foul dealing of any kind: God's truth shall be spoken, God's justice shall be done, on the throne called of St Peter: an honest Pope, Papa, or Father of Christendom, shall preside there. And such a throne of St Peter; and such a Christendom, for an honest Papa to preside in! The European populations everywhere hailed the omen; with shouting and rejoicing, leading-articles and tar-barrels; thinking people listened with astonishment,—not with sorrow if they were faithful or wise; with awe rather as at the heralding of death, and with a joy as of victory beyond death! Something pious, grand, and as if awful in that joy, revealing once more the Presence of a Divine Justice in this world. For, to such men, it was very clear how this poor devoted Pope would prosper, with his New Testament in his hand. An alarming business, that of governing in the throne of St Peter by the rule of veracity! By the rule of veracity, the so-called throne of St Peter was openly declared, above three hundred years ago, to be a falsity, a huge mistake, a pestilent dead carcass, which this Sun was weary of. More than three hundred years ago, the throne of St Peter received peremptory judicial notice to quit; authentic order, registered in Heaven's chancery and since legible in the hearts of all brave men, to take itself away,—to begone, and let us have no more to do with *it* and its delusions and impious deliriums;—and it has been sitting every day since, it may depend upon it, at its own peril withal, and will have to pay exact damages yet for every day it has so sat. Law of veracity? What this Popedom had to do by the law of veracity, was to give up its foul galvanic life, an offence to gods and men; honestly to die, and get itself buried!

Far from this was the thing the poor Pope undertook in regard to it;—and yet on the whole it was essentially this too. "Reforming Pope?" said one of our acquaintance, often in those weeks, "Was there ever such a miracle? About to break up that huge imposthume too, by 'curing' it? Turgot and Necker were nothing to this. God is great; and when a scandal is to end, brings some devoted man to take charge of it in hope, not in despair!"—But cannot he reform? asked many simple persons;—to whom our friend in grim banter would reply: "Reform a Popedom,—hardly. A wretched old kettle, ruined from

top to bottom, and consisting mainly now of foul
grime and *rust*: stop the holes of it, as your ante-
cessors have been doing, with temporary putty, it
may hang together yet a while; begin to hammer at
it, solder at it, to what you call mend and rectify it,
—it will fall to sherds, as sure as rust is rust; go all
into nameless dissolution,—and the fat in the fire will
be a thing worth looking at, poor Pope!"— —So
accordingly it has proved. The poor Pope, amid felici-
tations and tar-barrels of various kinds, went on joy-
fully for a season: but he had awakened, he as no
other man could do, the sleeping elements; mothers
of the whirlwinds, conflagrations, earthquakes. Questions not very soluble at present, were even sages and
heroes set to solve them, began everywhere with new
emphasis to be asked. Questions which all official
men wished, and almost hoped, to postpone till
Doomsday. Doomsday itself *had* come; that was the
terrible truth!—

For, sure enough, if once the law of veracity be
acknowledged as the rule for human things, there will
not anywhere be want of work for the reformer; in
very few places do human things adhere quite closely
to that law! Here was the Papa of Christendom pro-
claiming that such was actually the case;—whereupon
all over Christendom such results as we have seen. The
Sicilians, I think, were the first notable body that set
about applying this new strange rule sanctioned by
the general Father; they said to themselves, We do
not by the law of veracity belong to Naples and these
Neapolitan Officials; we will, by favour of Heaven
and the Pope, be free of these. Fighting ensued; in-
surrection, fiercely maintained in the Sicilian Cities;

with much bloodshed, much tumult and loud noise,
vociferation extending through all newspapers and
countries. The effect of this, carried abroad by newspapers and rumour, was great in all places; greatest
perhaps in Paris, which for sixty years past has been
the City of Insurrections. The French People had
plumed themselves on being, whatever else they were
not, at least the chosen 'soldiers of liberty,' who took
the lead of all creatures in that pursuit, at least; and
had become, as their orators, editors and litterateurs
diligently taught them, a People whose bayonets were
sacred, a kind of Messiah People, saving a blind world
in its own despite, and earning for themselves a ter-
restrial and even celestial glory very considerable
indeed. And here were the wretched downtrodden
populations of Sicily risen to rival them, and threaten-
ing to take the trade out of their hand.

No doubt of it, this hearing continually of the very
Pope's glory as a Reformer, of the very Sicilians fighting divinely for liberty behind barricades,—must have
bitterly aggravated the feeling of every Frenchman,
as he looked around him, at home, on a Louis-
Philippism, which had become the scorn of all the
world. "*Ichabod*; is the glory departing from us?
Under the sun is nothing baser, by all accounts and
evidences, than the system of repression and corrup-
tion, of shameless dishonesty and unbelief in anything but human baseness, that we now live under.
The Italians, the very Pope have become apostles of
liberty, and France is—what is France!"—We know
what France suddenly became in the end of February
next; and by a clear enough genealogy, we can trace
a considerable share in that event to the good simple

Pope with the New Testament in his hand. An outbreak, or at least a radical change and even inversion
of affairs hardly to be achieved without an outbreak,
everybody felt was inevitable in France: but it had
been universally expected that France would as usual
take the initiative in that matter; and had there been
no reforming Pope, no insurrectionary Sicily, France
had certainly not broken out then and so, but only
afterwards and otherwise. The French explosion, not
anticipated by the cunningest men there on the spot
scrutinising it, burst up unlimited, complete, defying
computation or control.

Close following which, as if by sympathetic sub-
terranean electricities, all Europe exploded, boundless,
uncontrollable; and we had the year 1848, one of the
most singular, disastrous, amazing, and on the whole
humiliating years the European world ever saw. Not
since the irruption of the Northern Barbarians has
there been the like. Everywhere immeasurable Democracy rose monstrous, loud, blatant, inarticulate as
the voice of Chaos. Everywhere the Official holy-of-
holies was scandalously laid bare to dogs and the pro-
fane:—Enter, all the world, see what kind of Official
holy it is. Kings everywhere, and reigning persons,
stared in sudden horror, the voice of the whole world
bellowing in their ear, "Begone, ye imbecile hypo-
crites, histrios not heroes! Off with you, off!"—and,
what was peculiar and notable in this year for the first
time, the Kings all made haste to go, as if exclaiming,
"We *are* poor histrios, we sure enough;—did you
want heroes? Don't kill us; we couldn't help it!"
Not one of them turned round, and stood upon his
Kingship, as upon a right he could afford to die for,

or to risk his skin upon; by no manner of means.
That, I say, is the alarming peculiarity at present.
Democracy, on this new occasion, finds all Kings
conscious that they are but Playactors. The miserable
mortals, enacting their High Life Below Stairs, with
faith only that this Universe may perhaps be all a
phantasm and hypocrisis,—the truculent Constable
of the Destinies suddenly enters: "Scandalous Phantasms, what do *you* here? Are 'solemnly constituted
Impostors' the proper Kings of men? Did you think
the Life of Man was a grimacing dance of apes? To
be led always by the squeak of your paltry fiddle? Ye
miserable, this Universe is not an upholstery Puppet-
play, but a terrible God's Fact; and you, I think,
—had not you better be gone!" They fled precipi-
tately, some of them with what we may call an exqui-
site ignominy,—in terror of the treadmill or worse.
And everywhere the people, or the populace, take
their own government upon themselves; and open
'kinglessness,' what we call *anarchy*,—how happy if
it be anarchy *plus* a street-constable!—is everywhere
the order of the day. Such was the history, from
Baltic to Mediterranean, in Italy, France, Prussia,
Austria, from end to end of Europe, in those March
days of 1848. Since the destruction of the old Roman
Empire by inroad of the Northern Barbarians, I have
known nothing similar.

And so, then, there remained no King in Europe;
no King except the Public Haranguer, haranguing on
barrelhead, in leading-article; or getting himself ag-
gregated into a National Parliament to harangue. And
for about four months all France, and to a great degree
all Europe, rough-ridden by every species of delirium,

except happily the murderous for most part, was a
weltering mob, presided over by M. de Lamartine at
the Hôtel-de-Ville; a most eloquent fair-spoken lite-
rary gentleman, whom thoughtless persons took for
a prophet, priest and heaven-sent evangelist, and
whom a wise Yankee friend of mine discerned to
be properly 'the first stump-orator in the world,
standing too on the highest stump,—for the time.' A
sorrowful spectacle to men of reflection, during the
time he lasted, that poor M. de Lamartine; with
nothing in him but melodious wind and *soft sowder*,
which he and others took for something divine and
not diabolic! Sad enough: the eloquent latest im-
personation of Chaos-come-again; able to talk for
itself, and declare persuasively that *it* is Cosmos!
However, you have but to wait a little, in such cases;
all balloons do and must give up their gas in the pres-
sure of things, and are collapsed in a sufficiently
wretched manner before long.

And so in City after City, street-barricades are
piled, and truculent, more or less murderous insur-
rection begins; populace after populace rises, King
after King capitulates or absconds; and from end to
end of Europe Democracy has blazed up explosive,
much higher, more irresistible and less resisted than
ever before; testifying too sadly on what a bottomless
volcano, or universal powder-mine of most inflam-
mable mutinous chaotic elements, separated from us
by a thin earth-rind, Society with all its arrangements
and acquirements everywhere, in the present epoch,
rests! The kind of persons who excite or give signal
to such revolutions,—students, young men of letters,
advocates, editors, hot inexperienced enthusiasts, or

fierce and justly bankrupt desperadoes, acting everywhere on the discontent of the millions and blowing
it into flame,—might give rise to reflections as to the
character of our epoch. Never till now did young
men, and almost children, take such a command in
human affairs. A changed time since the word *Senior*
(Seigneur, or *Elder*) was first devised to signify 'lord,'
or superior;—as in all languages of men we find it to
have been! Not an honourable document this either,
as to the spiritual condition of our epoch. In times
when men love wisdom, the old man will ever be
venerable, and be venerated, and reckoned noble: in
times that love something else than wisdom, and indeed have little or no wisdom, and see little or none
to love, the old man will cease to be venerated;—and
looking more closely, also, you will find that in fact
he has ceased to be venerable, and has begun to be
contemptible; a foolish *boy* still, a boy without the
graces, generosities and opulent strength of young
boys. In these days, what of *lordship* or leadership is
still to be done, the youth must do it, not the mature
or aged man; the mature man, hardened into sceptical
egoism, knows no monition but that of his own frigid
cautions, avarices, mean timidities; and can lead nowhither towards an object that even seems noble.
But to return.

This mad state of matters will of course before long
allay itself, as it has everywhere begun to do; the
ordinary necessities of men's daily existence cannot
comport with it, and these, whatever else is cast aside,
will have their way. Some remounting,—very temporary remounting,—of the old machine, under new
colours and altered forms, will probably ensue soon

in most countries: the old histrionic Kings will be admitted back under conditions, under 'Constitutions,' with national Parliaments, or the like fashionable adjuncts; and everywhere the old daily life will try to begin again. But there is now no hope that such arrangements can be permanent; that they can be other than poor temporary makeshifts, which, if they try to fancy and make themselves permanent, will be displaced by new explosions recurring more speedily than last time. In such baleful oscillation, afloat as amid raging bottomless eddies and conflicting sea-currents, not steadfast as on fixed foundations, must European Society continue swaying; now disastrously tumbling, then painfully readjusting itself, at ever shorter intervals,—till once the *new* rock-basis does come to light, and the weltering deluges of mutiny, and of need to mutiny, abate again!

For universal *Democracy*, whatever we may think of it, has declared itself as an inevitable fact of the days in which we live; and he who has any chance to instruct, or lead, in his days must begin by admitting that: new street-barricades, and new anarchies, still more scandalous if still less sanguinary, must return and again return, till governing persons everywhere know and admit that. Democracy, it may be said everywhere, is here:—for sixty years now, ever since the grand or *First* French Revolution, that fact has been terribly announced to all the world; in message after message, some of them very terrible indeed; and now at last all the world ought really to believe it. That the world does believe it; that even Kings now as good as believe it, and know, or with just terror

surmise, that they are but temporary phantasm Playactors, and that Democracy is the grand, alarming,
imminent and indisputable Reality: this, among the
scandalous phases we witnessed in the last two years,
is a phasis full of hope: a sign that we are advancing
closer and closer to the very Problem itself, which it
will behove us to solve or die;—that all fighting and
campaigning and coalitioning in regard to the *existence*
of the Problem, is hopeless and superfluous henceforth. The gods have appointed it *so*; no Pitt, nor
body of Pitts or mortal creatures can appoint it otherwise. Democracy, sure enough, is here: one knows
not how long it will keep hidden underground even in
Russia;—and here in England, though we object to it
resolutely in the form of street-barricades and insurrectionary pikes, and decidedly will not open doors to
it on those terms, the tramp of its million feet is on all
streets and thoroughfares, the sound of its bewildered
thousandfold voice is in all writings and speakings, in
all thinkings and modes and activities of men: the soul
that does not now, with hope or terror, discern *it*, is
not the one we address on this occasion. What *is*
Democracy; this huge inevitable Product of the Destinies, which is everywhere the portion of our Europe
in these latter days? There lies the question for us.
Whence comes it, this universal big black Democracy;
whither tends it; what is the meaning of it? A meaning it must have, or it would not be here. If we can
find the right meaning of it, we may, wisely submit-
ting or wisely resisting and controlling, still hope to
live in the midst of it; if we cannot find the right
meaning, if we find only the wrong or no meaning in
it, to live will not be possible!—The whole social

wisdom of the Present Time is summoned, in the
name of the Giver of Wisdom, to make clear to itself,
and lay deeply to heart with an eye to strenuous valiant
practice and effort, what the meaning of this universal
revolt of the European Populations, which calls itself
Democracy, and decides to continue permanent,
may be.

Certainly it is a drama full of action, event fast following event; in which curiosity finds endless scope,
and there are interests at stake, enough to rivet the
attention of all men simple and wise. Whereat the idle
multitude lift up their voices, gratulating, celebrating
sky-high; in rhyme and prose announcement, more
than plentiful, that *now* the New Era, and long-
expected Year One of Perfect Human Felicity has
come. Glorious and immortal people, sublime French
citizens, heroic barricades; triumph of civil and religious liberty—O Heaven! one of the inevitablest
private miseries, to an earnest man in such circumstances, is this multitudinous efflux of oratory and
psalmody, from the universal foolish human throat;
drowning for the moment all reflection whatsoever,
except the sorrowful one that you are fallen in an evil,
heavy laden, long-eared age, and must resignedly bear
your part in the same. The front wall of your wretched
old crazy dwelling, long denounced by you to no purpose, having at last fairly folded itself over, and fallen
prostrate into the street, the floors, as may happen,
will still hang on by the mere beam-ends, and coher-
ency of old carpentry, though in a sloping direction,
and depend there till certain poor rusty nails and
wormeaten dovetailings give way:—but is it cheering,
in such circumstances, that the whole household burst

forth into celebrating the new joys of light and venti-
lation, liberty and picturesqueness of position, and
thank God that now they have got a house to their
mind? My dear household, cease singing and psalm-
odying; lay aside your fiddles, take out your work-
implements, if you have any; for I can say with confidence the laws of gravitation are still active, and
rusty nails, wormeaten dovetailings, and secret co-
herency of old carpentry, are not the best basis for a
household!—In the lanes of Irish cities, I have heard
say, the wretched people are sometimes found living,
and perilously boiling their potatoes, on such swing-
floors and inclined planes hanging on by the joist-ends;
but I did not hear that they sang very much in cele-
bration of such lodging. No, they slid gently about,
sat near the back wall, and perilously boiled their
potatoes, in silence for most part!—

High shouts of exultation, in every dialect, by every
vehicle of speech and writing, rise from far and near
over this last avatar of Democracy in 1848: and yet, to
wise minds, the first aspect it presents seems rather to
be one of boundless misery and sorrow. What can be
more miserable than this universal hunting out of the
high dignitaries, solemn functionaries, and potent,
grave and reverend signiors of the world; this stormful
rising up of the inarticulate dumb masses everywhere,
against those who pretended to be speaking for them
and guiding them? These guides, then, were mere
blind men only pretending to see? These rulers were
not ruling at all; they had merely got on the attributes
and clothes of rulers, and were surreptitiously draw-
ing the wages, while the work remained undone? The
Kings were Sham-Kings, playacting as at Drury Lane;

—and what were the people withal that took them for real?

It is probably the hugest disclosure of *falsity* in human things that was ever at one time made. These reverend Dignitaries that sat amid their far-shining symbols and long-sounding long-admitted professions, were mere Impostors, then? Not a true thing they were doing, but a false thing. The story they told men was a cunningly-devised fable; the gospels they preached to them were *not* an account of man's real position in this world, but an incoherent fabrication, of dead ghosts and unborn shadows, of traditions, cants, indolences, cowardices,—a falsity of falsities, which at last *ceases* to stick together. Wilfully and against their will, these high units of mankind were cheats, then; and the low millions who believed in them were dupes,—a kind of *inverse* cheats too, or they would not have believed in them so long. A universal *Bankruptcy of Imposture*; that may be the brief definition of it. Imposture everywhere declared once more to be contrary to Nature; nobody will change its word into an act any farther:—fallen insolvent; unable to keep its head up by these false pretences, or make its pot boil any more for the present! A more scandalous phenomenon, wide as Europe, never afflicted the face of the sun. Bankruptcy everywhere; foul ignominy, and the abomination of desolation, in all high places: odious to look upon, as the carnage of a battlefield on the morrow morning;—a massacre not of the innocents; we cannot call it a massacre of the innocents; but a universal tumbling of Impostors and of Impostures into the street!—

Such a spectacle, can we call it joyful? There is a

joy in it, to the wise man too; yes, but a joy full of awe, and as it were sadder than any sorrow,—like the vision of immortality, unattainable except through death and the grave! And yet who would not, in his heart of hearts, feel piously thankful that Imposture has fallen bankrupt? By all means let it fall bankrupt; in the name of God let it do so, with whatever misery to itself and to all of us. Imposture, be it known then, —known it must and shall be,—is hateful, unendurable to God and man. Let it understand this everywhere; and swiftly make ready for departure, wherever it yet lingers; and let it learn never to return, if possible! The eternal voices, very audibly again, are speaking to proclaim this message, from side to side of the world. Not a very cheering message, but a very indispensable one.

Alas, it is sad enough that Anarchy is here; that we are not permitted to regret its being here,—for who that had, for this divine Universe, an eye which was human at all, could wish that Shams of any kind, especially that Sham-Kings should continue? No: at all costs, it is to be prayed by all men that Shams may *cease*. Good Heavens, to what depths have we got, when this to many a man seems strange! Yet strange to many a man it does seem; and to many a solid Englishman wholesomely digesting his pudding among what are called the cultivated classes, it seems strange exceedingly; a mad ignorant notion, quite heterodox, and big with mere ruin. He has been used to decent forms long since fallen empty of meaning, to plausible modes, solemnities grown ceremonial,—what you in your iconoclast humour call shams,—all his life long; never heard that there was any harm in them, that there was any getting on without them. Did not cotton spin itself, beef grow, and groceries and spiceries come in from the East and the West, quite comfortably by the side of shams? Kings reigned, what they were pleased to call reigning; lawyers pleaded, bishops preached, and honourable members perorated; and to crown the whole, as if it were all real and no sham there, did not scrip continue saleable, and the banker pay in bullion, or paper with a metallic basis? "The greatest sham, I have always thought, is he that would destroy shams."

Even so. To such depth have *I*, the poor knowing person of this epoch, got;—almost below the level of lowest humanity, and down towards the state of apehood and oxhood! For never till in quite recent generations was such a scandalous blasphemy quietly set forth among the sons of Adam; never before did the creature called man believe generally in his heart that lies were the rule in this Earth; that in deliberate long-established lying could there be help or salvation for him, could there be at length other than hindrance and destruction for him. O Heavyside, my solid friend, this is the sorrow of sorrows: what on earth can become of us till this accursed enchantment, the general summary and consecration of delusions, be cast forth from the heart and life of one and all! Cast forth it will be; it must, or we are tending, at all moments,—whitherward I do not like to name. Alas, and the casting of it out, to what heights and what depths will it lead us, in the sad universe mostly of lies and shams and hollow phantasms (grown very ghastly now), in which, as in a safe home, we have lived this century or two! To heights and

depths of social and individual *divorce* from delusions,
—of 'reform' in right sacred earnest, of indispensable
amendment, and stern sorrowful abrogation and order
to depart,—such as cannot well be spoken at present;
as dare scarcely be thought at present; which nevertheless are very inevitable, and perhaps rather imminent several of them! Truly we have a heavy task
of work before us; and there is a pressing call that we
should seriously begin upon it, before it tumble into
an inextricable mass, in which there will be no working, but only suffering and hopelessly perishing!—

Or perhaps Democracy, which we announce as
now come, will itself manage it? Democracy, once
modelled into suffrages, furnished with ballotboxes
and suchlike, will itself accomplish the salutary universal change from Delusive to Real, and make a new
blessed world of us by and by?—To the great mass of
men, I am aware, the matter presents itself quite on
this hopeful side. Democracy they consider to *be* a
kind of 'Government.' The old model, formed long
since, and brought to perfection in England now two
hundred years ago, has proclaimed itself to all Nations
as the new healing for every woe: "Set up a Parliament," the Nations everywhere say, when the old
King is detected to be a Sham-King, and hunted out
or not; "set up a Parliament; let us have suffrages,
universal suffrages; and all either at once or by due
degrees will be right, and a real Millennium come!"
Such is their way of construing the matter.

Such, alas, is by no means my way of construing
the matter; if it were, I should have had the happiness of remaining silent, and been without call to

speak here. It is because the contrary of all this is
deeply manifest to me, and appears to be forgotten
by multitudes of my contemporaries, that I have had
to undertake addressing a word to them. The contrary of all this;—and the farther I look into the roots
of all this, the more hateful, ruinous and dismal does
the state of mind all this could have originated in
appear to me. To examine this recipe of a Parliament,
how fit it is for governing Nations, nay how fit it may
now be, in these new times, for governing England
itself where we are used to it so long: this, too, is an
alarming inquiry, to which all thinking men, and good
citizens of their country, who have an ear for the
small still voices and eternal intimations, across the
temporary clamours and loud blaring proclamations,
are now solemnly invited. Invited by the rigorous
fact itself; which will one day, and that perhaps soon,
demand practical decision or redecision of it from us,
—with enormous penalty if we decide it wrong! I
think we shall all have to consider this question, one
day; better perhaps now than later, when the leisure
may be less. If a Parliament, with suffrages and universal or any conceivable kind of suffrages, *is* the
method, then certainly let us set about discovering
the kind of suffrages, and rest no moment till we have
got them. But it is possible that a Parliament may
not be the method! Possible the inveterate notions
of the English People may have settled it as the
method, and the Everlasting Laws of Nature may
have settled it as not the method! Not the whole
method; nor the method at all, if taken as the whole?
If a Parliament with never such suffrages is *not* the
method settled by this latter authority, then it will

urgently behove us to become aware of that fact, and to quit such method;—we may depend upon it, however unanimous *we* be, every step taken in that direction will, by the Eternal Law of things, be a step *from* improvement, not towards it.

Not towards it, I say, if so! Unanimity of voting, —that will do nothing for us if *so*. Your ship cannot double Cape Horn by its excellent plans of voting. The ship may vote this and that, above decks and below, in the most harmonious exquisitely constitutional manner: the ship, to get round Cape Horn, will find a set of conditions already voted for, and fixed with adamantine rigour by the ancient Elemental Powers, who are entirely careless how you vote. If you can, by voting or without voting, ascertain these conditions, and valiantly conform to them, you will get round the Cape: if you cannot,—the ruffian Winds will blow you ever back again; the inexorable Icebergs, dumb privy-councillors from Chaos, will nudge you with most chaotic 'admonition;' you will be flung half-frozen on the Patagonian cliffs, or admonished into shivers by your iceberg councillors, and sent sheer down to Davy Jones, and will never get round Cape Horn at all! Unanimity on board ship; —yes indeed, the ship's crew may be very unanimous, which doubtless, for the time being, will be very comfortable to the ship's crew, and to their Phantasm Captain if they have one: but if the tack they unanimously steer upon is guiding them into the belly of the Abyss, it will not profit them much!—Ships accordingly do not use the ballotbox at all; and they reject the Phantasm species of Captains: one wishes much some other Entities,—since all entities lie under the same rigorous set of laws,—could be brought to shew as much wisdom, and sense at least of self-preservation, the *first* command of Nature. Phantasm Captains with unanimous votings: this is considered to be all the law and all the prophets, at present.

If a man could shake out of his mind the universal noise of political doctors in this generation and in the last generation or two, and consider the matter face to face, with his own sincere intelligence looking at it, I venture to say he would find this a very extra-ordinary method of navigating, whether in the Straits of Magellan or the undiscovered Sea of Time. To prosper in this world, to gain felicity, victory and im-provement, either for a man or a nation, there is but one thing requisite, That the man or nation can dis-cern what the true regulations of the Universe are in regard to him and his pursuit, and can faithfully and steadfastly follow these. These will lead him to victory; whoever it may be that sets him in the way of these, —were it Russian Autocrat, Chartist Parliament, Grand Lama, Force of Public Opinion, Archbishop of Canterbury, M'Croudy the Seraphic Doctor with his Last-evangel of Political Economy,—sets him in the sure way to please the Author of this Universe, and is his friend of friends. And again, whoever does the contrary is, for a like reason, his enemy of enemies. This may be taken as fixed.

And now by what method ascertain the monition of the gods in regard to our affairs? How decipher, with best fidelity, the eternal regulation of the Uni-verse; and read, from amid such confused embroil-ments of human clamour and folly, what the real Divine Message to us is? A divine message, or eternal

regulation of the Universe, there verily is, in regard
to every conceivable procedure and affair of man:
faithfully following this, said procedure or affair will
prosper, and have the whole Universe to second it,
and carry it, across the fluctuating contradictions, towards a victorious goal; not following this, mistaking
this, disregarding this, destruction and wreck are certain for every affair. How find it? All the world
answers me, "Count heads; ask Universal Suffrage,
by the ballotboxes, and that will tell." Universal suffrage, ballotboxes, count of heads? Well,—I perceive
we have got into strange spiritual latitudes indeed.
Within the last half century or so, either the Universe
or else the heads of men must have altered very much.
Half a century ago, and down from Father Adam's
time till then, the Universe, wherever I could hear
tell of it, was wont to be of somewhat abstruse nature;
by no means carrying its secret written on its face,
legible to every passer-by; on the contrary, obstinately
hiding its secret from all foolish, slavish, wicked, in-
sincere persons, and partially disclosing it to the wise
and noble-minded alone, whose number was not the
majority in my time!—Or perhaps the chief end of
man being now, in these improved epochs, to make
money and spend it, his interests in the Universe have
become amazingly simplified of late; capable of being
voted on with effect by almost anybody? 'To buy in
the cheapest market, and sell in the dearest:' truly if
that is the summary of his social duties, and the final
divine-message he has to follow, we may trust him
extensively to vote upon that. But if it is *not*, and
never was, or can be? If the Universe will not carry
on its divine bosom any commonwealth of mortals

that have no higher aim,—being still 'a Temple and Hall of Doom,' not a mere Weaving-shop and Cattle-pen? If the unfathomable Universe has decided to *reject* Human Beavers pretending to be Men; and will abolish, pretty rapidly perhaps, in hideous mud-deluges, their 'markets' and them, unless they think of it?—In that case it were better to think of it; and the Democracies and Universal Suffrages, I can observe, will require to modify themselves a good deal!

Historically speaking, I believe there was no Nation that could subsist upon Democracy. Of ancient Republics, and *Demoi* and *Populi*, we have heard much; but it is now pretty well admitted to be nothing to our purpose;—a universal-suffrage republic, or a general-suffrage one, or any but a most limited-suffrage one, never came to light, or dreamed of doing so, in ancient times. When the mass of the population were slaves, and the voters intrinsically a kind of *kings*, or men born to rule others; when the voters were *real* 'aristocrats' and manageable dependants of such,—then doubtless voting, and confused jumbling of talk and intrigue, might, without immediate destruction, or the need of a Cavaignac to intervene with cannon and sweep the streets clear of it, go on; and beautiful developments of manhood might be possible beside it, for a season. Beside it; or even, if you will, by means of it, and in virtue of it, though that is by no means so certain as is often supposed. Alas, no: the reflective constitutional mind has misgivings as to the origin of old Greek and Roman nobleness; and indeed knows not how this or any other human nobleness could well be 'originated,' or brought to pass, by voting or without voting, in this world, except by the grace of God very mainly;—and remembers, with a sigh, that of the Seven Sages themselves no fewer than three were bits of Despotic Kings, Τύραννοι, 'Tyrants' so-called (such being greatly wanted there); and that the other four were very far from Red Republicans, if of any political faith whatever! We may quit the Ancient Classical concern, and leave it to College clubs and speculative debating societies, in these late days.

Of the various French Republics that have been tried, or that are still on trial,—of these also it is not needful to say any word. But there is one modern instance of Democracy nearly perfect, the Republic of the United States, which has actually subsisted for three-score years or more, with immense success as is affirmed; to which many still appeal, as to a sign of hope for all nations, and a 'Model Republic.' Is not America an instance in point? Why should not all Nations subsist and flourish on Democracy, as America does?

Of America it would ill beseem any Englishman, and me perhaps as little as another, to speak unkindly, to speak *unpatriotically*, if any of us even felt so. Sure enough, America is a great, and in many respects a blessed and hopeful phenomenon. Sure enough, these hardy millions of Anglosaxon men prove themselves worthy of their genealogy; and, with the axe and plough and hammer, if not yet with any much finer kind of implements, are triumphantly clearing out wide spaces, seedfields for the sustenance and refuge of mankind, arenas for the future history of the world;—doing, in their day and generation, a creditable and cheering feat under the sun. But as to a Model Republic, or a model anything, the wise among themselves know too well that there is nothing to be said. Nay, the title hitherto to be a Commonwealth or Nation at all, among the ἔθνοι of the world, is, strictly considered, still a thing they are but striving for, and indeed have not yet done much towards attaining. Their Constitution, such as it may be, was made here, not there; went over with them from the Old-Puritan English workshop, ready-made. Deduct what they carried with them from England ready-made,—their common English Language, and that same Constitution, or rather elixir of constitutions, their inveterate and now, as it were, inborn reverence for the Constable's Staff; two quite immense attainments, which England had to spend much blood, and valiant sweat of brow and brain, for centuries long, in achieving;—and what new elements of polity or nationhood, what noble new phasis of human arrangement, or social device worthy of Prometheus or of Epimetheus, yet comes to light in America? Cotton-crops and Indian corn and dollars come to light; and half a world of untilled land, where populations that respect the constable can live, for the present, *without* Government: this comes to light; and the profound sorrow of all nobler hearts, here uttering itself as silent patient unspeakable ennui, there coming out as vague elegiac wailings, that there is still next to nothing more. 'Anarchy *plus* a street-constable:' that also is anarchic to me, and other than quite lovely!

I foresee too that, long before the waste lands are full, the very street-constable, on these poor terms, will have become impossible: without the waste lands, as here in our Europe, I do not see how he could continue possible many weeks. Cease to brag to me of America, and its model institutions and constitutions. To men in their sleep there is nothing granted in this world: nothing, or as good as nothing, to men that sit idly *caucusing* and ballotboxing on the graves of their heroic ancestors, saying, "It is well, it is well!" Corn and bacon are granted: not a very sublime boon, on such conditions; a boon moreover which, on such conditions, cannot last! No: America too will have to strain its energies, in quite other fashion than this; to crack its sinews, and all but break its heart, as the rest of us have had to do, in thousandfold wrestle with the Pythons and mud-demons, before it can become a habitation for the gods. America's battle is yet to fight; and we, sorrowful though nothing doubting, will wish her strength for it. New Spiritual Pythons, plenty of them; enormous Megatherions, as ugly as were ever born of mud, loom huge and hideous out of the twilight Future on America; and she will have her own agony, and her own victory, but on other terms than she is yet quite aware of. Hitherto she but ploughs and hammers, in a very successful manner; hitherto, in spite of her 'roast-goose with apple-sauce,' she is not much. 'Roast-goose with apple-sauce for the poorest working man:' well surely that is something,—thanks to your respect for the street-constable, and to your continents of fertile waste land;—but that, even if it could continue, is by no means enough; that is not even an instalment towards what will be required of you. My friend, brag not yet of our American cousins! Their quantity of cotton, dollars, industry and resources, I believe to be almost unspeakable; but I can by no means worship the like of these. What great human soul, what great thought, what great noble thing that one could worship, or loyally admire, has yet been produced there? None; the American cousins have yet done none of these things. "What they have done?" growls Smelfungus, tired of the subject: "They have doubled their population every twenty years. They have begotten, with a rapidity beyond recorded example, Eighteen Millions of the greatest *bores* ever seen in this world before,—that, hitherto, is their feat in History!"—And so we leave them, for the present; and cannot predict the success of Democracy, on this side of the Atlantic, from their example.

Alas, on this side of the Atlantic and on that, Democracy, we apprehend, is forever impossible! So much, with certainty of loud astonished contradiction from all manner of men at present, but with sure appeal to the Law of Nature and the ever-abiding Fact, may be suggested and asserted once more. The Universe itself is a Monarchy and Hierarchy; large liberty of 'voting' there, all manner of choice, utmost free-will, but with conditions inexorable and immeasurable annexed to every exercise of the same. A most free commonwealth of 'voters;' but with Eternal Justice to preside over it, Eternal Justice enforced by Almighty Power! This is the model of 'constitutions;' this: nor in any Nation where there has not yet (in some supportable and withal some constantly-increasing degree) been confided to the *Noblest*, with his select series of *Nobler*, the divine everlasting duty of directing and controlling the Ignoble, has the 'Kingdom of God,' which we all pray for, 'come,' nor can 'His will' even *tend* to be 'done on Earth as it is in Heaven' till then. My Christian friends, and indeed my Sham-Christian and Anti-Christian, and all manner of men, are invited to reflect on this. They will find it to be the truth of the case. The Noble in the high place, the Ignoble in the low; that is, in all times and in all places, the Almighty Maker's Law.

To raise the Sham-Noblest, and solemnly consecrate *him* by whatever method, new-devised, or slavishly adhered to from old wont, this, little as we may regard it, is a practical blasphemy forevermore, and Nature will in no wise forget it. Alas, there lies the origin, the fatal necessity, of modern Democracy everywhere. It is the Noblest, not the Sham-Noblest; it is God Almighty's Noble, not the Court-Tailor's Noble, nor the Able-Editor's Noble, that must, in some approximate degree, be raised to the supreme place; he and not a counterfeit,—under penalties! Penalties deep as death, and at length terrible as hell-on-earth, my constitutional friend!—Will the ballotbox raise the Noblest to the chief place; does any sane man deliberately believe such a thing? That nevertheless is the indispensable result, attain it how we may: if that is attained, all is attained; if not that, nothing. He that cannot believe the ballotbox to be attaining it, will be comparatively indifferent to the ballotbox. Excellent for keeping the ship's crew at peace, under their Phantasm Captain; but unserviceable, under such, for getting round Cape Horn. Alas, that there should be human beings requiring to have these things argued of, at this late time of day!

I say, it is the everlasting privilege of the foolish to

be governed by the wise; to be guided in the right
path by those who know it better than they. This is
the first 'right of man;' compared with which all other
rights are as nothing,—mere superfluities, corollaries
which will follow of their own accord out of this;
if they be not contradictions to this, and less than
nothing! To the wise it is not a privilege; far other
indeed. Doubtless, as bringing preservation to their
country, it implies preservation of themselves withal;
but intrinsically it is the harshest duty a wise man, if
he be indeed wise, has laid to his hand. A duty which
he would fain enough shirk; which accordingly, in
these sad times of doubt and cowardly sloth, he has
long everywhere been endeavouring to reduce to its
minimum, and has in fact in most cases nearly escaped
altogether. It is an ungoverned world; a world which
we flatter ourselves will henceforth need no governing. On the dust of our heroic ancestors we too sit
ballotboxing, saying to one another, It is well, it is
well! By inheritance of their noble struggles, we have
been permitted to sit slothful so long. By noble toil,
not by shallow laughter and vain talk, they made this
English Existence from a savage forest into an arable
inhabitable field for us; and we idly dreaming it would
grow spontaneous crops forever,—find it now in a too
questionable state; peremptorily requiring real labour
and agriculture again. Real 'agriculture' is not plea-
sant; much pleasanter to reap and winnow (with
ballotbox or otherwise) than to plough!

Who would govern that can get along without governing? He that is fittest for it, is of all men the un-
willingest unless constrained. By multifarious devices
we have been endeavouring to dispense with govern-

ing; and by very superficial speculations, of *laissez-faire*, supply-and-demand, &c. &c. to persuade ourselves that it is best so. The Real Captain, unless it be some Captain of mechanical Industry hired by Mammon, where is he in these days? Most likely, in silence, in sad isolation somewhere, in remote obscurity; trying if, in an evil ungoverned time, he cannot at least govern himself. The Real Captain undiscoverable; the Phantasm Captain everywhere very conspicuous:—it is thought Phantasm Captains, aided by ballotboxes, are the true method, after all. They are much the pleasantest for the time being! And so no *Dux* or Duke of any sort, in any province of our affairs, now *leads*: the Duke's Bailiff *leads*, what little leading is required for getting in the rents; and the Duke merely rides in the state coach. It is everywhere so: and now at last we see a world all rushing towards strange consummations, because it is and has long been so!

I do not suppose any reader of mine, or many persons in England at all, have much faith in Fraternity, Equality and the Revolutionary Millenniums preached by the French Prophets in this age: but there are many movements here too which tend inevitably in the like direction; and good men, who would stand aghast at Red Republic and its adjuncts, seem to me travelling at full speed towards that or a similar goal! Certainly the notion everywhere prevails among us too, and preaches itself abroad in every dialect, uncontradicted anywhere so far as I can hear, That the grand panacea for social woes is what we call 'enfranchisement,' 'emancipation;' or, translated into practical language, the cutting asunder of human relations, wherever they are found grievous, as is like to be pretty universally the case at the rate we have been going for some generations past. Let us all be 'free' of one another; we shall then be happy. Free, without bond or connexion except that of cash payment; fair day's wages for the fair day's work; bargained for by voluntary contract, and law of supply and demand: this is thought to be the true solution of all difficulties and injustices that have occurred between man and man.

To rectify the relation that exists between two men, is there no method, then, but that of ending it? The old relation has become unsuitable, obsolete, perhaps unjust; it imperatively requires to be amended; and the remedy is, Abolish it, let there henceforth be no relation at all. From the 'Sacrament of Marriage' downwards, human beings used to be manifoldly related, one to another, and each to all; and there was no relation among human beings, just or unjust, that had not its grievances and difficulties, its necessities on both sides to bear and forbear. But henceforth, be it known, we have changed all that, by favour of Heaven: 'the voluntary principle' has come up, which will itself do the business for us; and now let a new Sacrament, that of *Divorce*, which we call emancipation, and spout of on our platforms, be universally the order of the day!—Have men considered whither all this is tending, and what it certainly enough betokens? Cut every human relation which has anywhere grown uneasy sheer asunder; reduce whatsoever was compulsory to voluntary, whatsoever was permanent

among us to the condition of nomadic:—in other
words, loosen by assiduous wedges in every joint, the
whole fabric of social existence, stone from stone; till
at last, all now being loose enough, it can, as we
already see in most countries, be overset by sudden
outburst of revolutionary rage; and, lying as mere
mountains of anarchic rubbish, solicit you to sing
Fraternity, &c. over it, and to rejoice in the new re-
markable era of human progress we have arrived at.

Certainly Emancipation proceeds with rapid strides
among us, this good while; and has got to such a
length as might give rise to reflections in men of a
serious turn. West-Indian Blacks are emancipated,
and it appears refuse to work: Irish Whites have long
been entirely emancipated; and nobody asks them to
work, or on condition of finding them potatoes (which,
of course, is indispensable), permits them to work.
—Among speculative persons, a question has sometimes risen: In the progress of Emancipation, are we
to look for a time when all the Horses also are to be
emancipated, and brought to the supply-and-demand
principle? Horses too have 'motives;' are acted on
by hunger, fear, hope, love of oats, terror of platted
leather; nay they have vanity, ambition, emulation,
thankfulness, vindictiveness; some rude outline of all
our human spiritualities,—a rude resemblance to us
in mind and intelligence, even as they have in bodily
frame. The Horse, poor dumb four-footed fellow, he
too has his private feelings, his affections, gratitudes;
and deserves good usage; no human master, without
crime, shall treat his unjustly either, or recklessly lay
on the whip where it is not needed:—I am sure if I
could make him 'happy,' I should be willing to grant

a small vote (in addition to the late twenty millions) for that object!

Him too you occasionally tyrannise over; and with bad result to yourselves among others; using the leather in a tyrannous unnecessary manner; withholding, or scantily furnishing, the oats and ventilated stabling that are due. Rugged horse-subduers, one fears they are a little tyrannous at times. "Am I not a horse, and *half*-brother?"—To remedy which, so far as remediable, fancy—the horses all 'emancipated;' restored to their primeval right of property in the grass of this Globe; turned out to graze in an independent supply-and-demand manner! So long as grass lasts, I dare say they are very happy, or think themselves so. And Farmer Hodge sallying forth, on a dry spring morning, with a sieve of oats in his hand, and agony of eager expectation in his heart, is he happy? Help me to plough this day, Black Dobbin: oats in full measure if thou wilt. "Hlunh, No— thank!" snorts Black Dobbin; he prefers glorious liberty and the grass. Bay Darby, wilt not thou perhaps? "Hlunh!"—Grey Joan, then, my beautiful broad-bottomed mare,—O Heaven, she too answers Hlunh! Not a quadruped of them will plough a stroke for me. Corn-crops are *ended* in this world!—For the sake, if not of Hodge, then of Hodge's horses, one prays this benevolent practice might now cease, and a new and better one try to begin. Small kindness to Hodge's horses to emancipate them! The fate of all emancipated horses is, sooner or later, inevitable. To have in this habitable Earth no grass to eat,—in Black Jamaica gradually none, as in White Connemara already none;—to roam aimless, wasting the seedfields of the world; and be hunted home to Chaos, by the due watch-dogs and due hell-dogs, with such horrors of forsaken wretchedness as were never seen before! These things are not sport; they are terribly true, in this country at this hour.

Between our Black West Indies and our White Ireland, between these two extremes of lazy refusal to work, and of famishing inability to find any work, what a world have we made of it, with our fierce Mammon-worships, and our benevolent philander-ings, and idle godless nonsenses of one kind and another! Supply-and-demand, Leave-it-alone, Volun-tary principle, Time will mend it:—till British in-dustrial existence seems fast becoming one huge poison-swamp of reeking pestilence physical and moral; a hideous *living* Golgotha of souls and bodies buried alive; such a Curtius' gulf, communicating with the Nether Deeps, as the Sun never saw till now. These scenes, which the *Morning Chronicle* is bring-ing home to all minds of men,—thanks to it for a service such as Newspapers have seldom done,—ought to excite unspeakable reflections in every mind. Thirty-thousand outcast Needlewomen working them-selves swiftly to death; three-million Paupers rotting in forced idleness, *helping* said Needlewomen to die: these are but items in the sad ledger of despair.

Thirty-thousand wretched women, sunk in that putrefying well of abominations; they have oozed in upon London, from the universal Stygian quagmire of British industrial life; are accumulated in the *well* of the concern, to that extent. British charity is smitten to the heart, at the laying bare of such a scene;

passionately undertakes, by enormous subscription of money, or by other enormous effort, to redress that individual horror; as I and all men hope it may. But, alas, what next? This general well and cesspool once baled clean out to-day, will begin before night to fill itself anew. The universal Stygian quagmire is still there; opulent in women ready to be ruined, and in men ready. Towards the same sad cesspool will these waste currents of human ruin ooze and gravitate as heretofore; except in draining the universal quagmire itself there is no remedy. "And for that, what is the method?" cry many in an angry manner. To whom, for the present, I answer only, "Not 'emancipation,' it would seem, my friends; not the cutting loose of human ties, something far the reverse of that!"

Many things have been written about shirtmaking; but here perhaps is the saddest thing of all, not written anywhere till now, that I know of. Shirts by the thirty-thousand are made at twopence-halfpenny each;—and in the meanwhile no needlewoman, distressed or other, can be procured in London by any housewife to give, for fair wages, fair help in sewing. Ask any thrifty house-mother, high or low, and she will answer. In high houses and in low, there is the same answer: no *real* needlewoman, 'distressed' or other, has been found attainable in any of the houses I frequent. Imaginary needlewomen, who demand considerable wages, and have a deepish appetite for beer and viands, I hear of everywhere; but their sewing proves too often a distracted puckering and botching; not sewing, only the fallacious hope of it, a fond imagination of the mind. Good sempstresses are to be hired in every village; and in London, with its famishing thirty-thousand, not at all, or hardly.—Is not No-government beautiful in human business? To such length has the Leave-alone principle carried it, by way of organising labour, in this affair of shirt-making. Let us hope the Leave-alone principle has now got its apotheosis; and taken wing towards higher regions than ours, to deal henceforth with a class of affairs more appropriate for it!

Reader, did you ever hear of 'Constituted Anarchy?' Anarchy; the choking, sweltering, deadly and killing rule of No-rule; the consecration of cupidity, and braying folly, and dim stupidity and baseness, in most of the affairs of men? Slop-shirts attainable three-halfpence cheaper, by the ruin of living bodies and immortal souls? Solemn Bishops and high Dignitaries, *our* divine 'Pillars of Fire by night,' debating meanwhile, with their largest wigs and gravest look, upon something they call 'prevenient grace?' Alas, our noble men of genius, Heaven's *real* messengers to us, they also rendered nearly futile by the wasteful time;—preappointed they everywhere, and assiduously trained by all their pedagogues and monitors, to 'rise in Parliament,' to compose orations, write books, or in short speak *words*, for the approval of reviewers; instead of doing real kingly *work* to be approved of by the gods! Our 'Government,' a highly 'responsible' one; responsible to no God that I can hear of, but to the twenty-seven million *gods* of the shilling gallery. A Government tumbling and drifting on the whirlpools and mud-deluges, floating atop in a conspicuous manner, nowhither,—like the carcass of a drowned ass. Authentic *Chaos* come up into this sunny Cosmos again; and all men singing *Gloria in excelsis* to it. In spirituals and temporals, in field and workshop, from Manchester to Dorsetshire, from Lambeth Palace to the Lanes of Whitechapel, wherever men meet and toil and traffic together,—Anarchy, Anarchy; and only the street-constable (though with ever-increasing difficulty) still maintaining himself in the middle of it; that so, for one thing, this blessed exchange of slop-shirts for the souls of women may transact itself in a peaceable manner!—I, for my part, do profess myself in eternal opposition to this, and discern well that universal Ruin has us in the wind, unless we can get out of this. My friend Crabbe, in a late number of his *Intermittent Radiator*, pertinently enough exclaims:

'When shall we have done with all this of British Liberty, Voluntary Principle, Dangers of Centralisation, and the like? It is really getting too bad. For British Liberty, it seems, the people cannot be taught to read. British Liberty, shuddering to interfere with the rights of capital, takes six or eight millions of money annually to feed the idle labourer whom it dare not employ. For British Liberty we live over poisonous cesspools, gully-drains, and detestable abominations; and omnipotent London cannot sweep the dirt out of itself. British Liberty produces—what? Floods of Hansard Debates every year, and apparently little else at present. If these are the results of British Liberty, I, for one, move we should lay it on the shelf a little, and look out for something other and farther. We have achieved British Liberty hundreds of years ago; and are fast growing, on the strength of it, one of the most absurd populations the Sun, among his great Museum of Absurdities, looks down upon at present.'

Curious enough: the model of the world just now is England and her Constitution; all Nations striving towards it; poor France swimming these last sixty years in seas of horrid dissolution and confusion, resolute to attain this blessedness of free voting, or to die in chase of it. Prussia too, solid Germany itself, has all broken out into crackling of musketry, loud pamphleteering and Frankfort parliamenting and palavering; Germany too will scale the sacred mountains, how steep soever, and, by talisman of ballotbox, inhabit a political Elysium henceforth. All the Nations have that one hope. Very notable, and rather sad to the humane onlooker. For it is sadly conjectured, all the Nations labour somewhat under a mistake as to England, and the causes of her freedom and her prosperous cotton-spinning; and have much misread the nature of her Parliament, and the effect of ballotboxes and universal-suffrages there.

What if it were because the English Parliament was from the first, and is only just now ceasing to be, a Council of actual Rulers, real Governing Persons (called Peers, Mitred Abbots, Lords, Knights of the Shire, or howsoever called), actually *ruling* each his section of the country,—and possessing (it must be said) in the lump, or when assembled as a Council, uncommon patience, devoutness, probity, discretion and good fortune,—that the said Parliament ever came to be good for much? In that case it will not be easy to 'imitate' the English Parliament; and the ballotbox and suffrage will be the mere bow of Robin Hood, which it is given to very few to bend, or shoot with to any perfection. And if the Peers become mere big Capitalists, Railway Directors, gigantic Hucksters,

Kings of Scrip, *without* lordly quality, or other virtue
except cash; and the Mitred Abbots change to mere
Able-Editors, masters of Parliamentary Eloquence,
Doctors of Political Economy, and suchlike; and all
have to be elected by a universal-suffrage ballotbox,
—I do not see how the English Parliament itself will
long continue sea-worthy! Nay, I find England, in
her own big dumb heart, wherever you come upon
her in a silent meditative hour, begins to have dreadful
misgivings about it.

The model of the world, then, is at once unattainable by the world, and not much worth attaining?
England, as I read the omens, is now called a second
time to 'shew the Nations how to live;' for by her
Parliament, as chief governing entity, I fear she is not
long for this world! Poor England must herself again,
in these new strange times, the old methods being
quite worn out, 'learn how to live.' That now is the
terrible problem for England, as for all the Nations;
and she alone of all, not *yet* sunk into open Anarchy,
but left with time for repentance and amendment;
she, wealthiest of all in material resource, in spiritual
energy, in ancient loyalty to law, and in the qualities
that yield such loyalty,—she perhaps alone of all may
be able, with huge travail, and the strain of all her
faculties, to accomplish some solution. She will have
to try it, she has now to try it; she must accomplish
it, or perish from her place in the world!

England, as I persuade myself, still contains in it
many *kings*; possesses, as Old Rome did, many men
not needing 'election' to command, but eternally
elected for it by the Maker Himself. England's one
hope is in these, just now. They are among the silent,

I believe; mostly far away from platforms and public palaverings; not speaking forth the image of their nobleness in transitory words, but imprinting it, each on his own little section of the world, in silent facts, in modest valiant actions, that will endure forevermore. They must sit silent no longer. They are summoned to assert themselves; to act forth, and articulately vindicate, in the teeth of howling multitudes, of a world too justly *maddened* into all manner of delirious clamours, what of wisdom they derive from God. England, and the Eternal Voices, summon them; poor England never so needed them as now. Up, be doing everywhere: the hour of crisis has verily come! In all sections of English life, the godmade *king* is needed; is pressingly demanded in most; in some, cannot longer, without peril as of conflagration, be dispensed with. He, wheresoever he finds himself, can say, "Here too am I wanted; here is the kingdom I have to subjugate, and introduce God's laws into,—God's Laws, instead of Mammon's and M'Croudy's, and the Old Anarch's! Here is my work, here or nowhere."— —Are there many such, who will answer to the call, in England? It turns on that, whether England, rapidly crumbling in these very years and months, shall go down to the Abyss as her neighbours have all done, or survive to new grander destinies *without* solution of continuity! Probably the chief question of the world at present.

The true 'commander' and king: he who knows for himself the divine Appointments of this Universe, the Eternal Laws ordained by God the Maker, in conforming to which lies victory and felicity, in departing from which lies, and forever must lie, sorrow and

defeat, for each and all of the Posterity of Adam in
every time and every place; he who has sworn fealty
to these, and dare alone against the world assert these,
and dare not with the whole world at his back deflect
from these;—he, I know too well, is a rare man.
Difficult to discover; not quite discoverable, I apprehend, by manœuvring of ballotboxes, and riddling of
the popular clamour according to the most approved
methods. He is not sold at any shop I know of,—
though sometimes, as at the sign of the Ballotbox, he
is advertised for sale. Difficult indeed to discover:
and not very much assisted, or encouraged in late
times, to discover *himself*;—which, I think, might be
a kind of help? Encouraged rather, and commanded
in all ways, if he be wise, to *hide* himself, and give
place to the windy Counterfeit of himself; such as the
universal-suffrages can recognise, such as loves the
most sweet voices of the universal suffrages!—O
Peter, what becomes of such a People; what can
become?

Did you never hear, with the mind's ear as well,
that fateful Hebrew Prophecy, I think the fatefullest
of all, which sounds daily through the streets, "Ou'
clo! Ou' clo!"—A certain People, once upon a time,
clamorously voted by overwhelming majority, "Not
he; Barabbas, not he! *Him*, and what he is, and what
he deserves, we know well enough: a reviler of the
Chief Priests and sacred Chancery wigs; a seditious
Heretic, physical-force Chartist, and enemy of his
country and mankind: To the gallows and the cross
with him! Barabbas is our man; Barabbas, we are
for Barabbas!" They got Barabbas:—have you well
considered what a fund of purblind obduracy, of

opaque *flunkeyism* grown truculent and transcendent; what an eye for the phylacteries, and want of eye for the eternal noblenesses; sordid loyalty to the prosperous Semblances, and high-treason against the Supreme Fact, such a vote betokens in these natures? For it was the consummation of a long series of such; they and their fathers had long kept voting so. A singular People; who could both produce such divine men, and then could so stone and crucify them: a People terrible from the beginning!—Well, they got Barabbas; and they got, of course, such guidance as Barabbas and the like of him could give them; and, of course, they stumbled ever downwards and devilwards, in their truculent stiffnecked way; and—and, at this hour, after eighteen centuries of sad fortune, they prophetically sing "Ou' clo!" in all the cities of the world. Might the world, at this late hour, but take note of them, and understand their song a little!—

Yes, there are some things the universal-suffrage can decide,—and about these it will be exceedingly useful to consult the universal-suffrage: but in regard to most things of importance, and in regard to the choice of men especially, there is (astonishing as it may seem) next to no capability on the part of universal-suffrage.—I request all candid persons, who have never so little originality of mind, and every man has a little, to consider this. If true, it involves such a change in our now fashionable modes of procedure as fills me with astonishment and alarm. *If* popular suffrage is not the way of ascertaining what the Laws of the Universe are, and who it is that will best guide us in the way of these,—then woe is to us if we do not take another method. Delolme on the British

Constitution will not save us; deaf will the Parcæ be to votes of the House, to leading articles, constitutional philosophies. The other method—alas, it involves a stopping short, or vital change of direction, in the glorious career which all Europe, with shouts heaven-high, is now galloping along: and that, happen when it may, will, to many of us, be probably a rather surprising business!

One thing I do know, and can again assert with great confidence, supported by the whole Universe, and by some Two Hundred generations of men, who have left us some record of themselves there, That the few Wise will have, by one method or another, to take command of the innumerable Foolish; that they must be got to take it;—and that, in fact, since Wisdom, which means also valour and heroic Nobleness, is alone strong in this world, and one wise man is stronger than all men unwise, they can be got. That they must take it; and having taken, must keep it, and do their God's-Message in it, and defend the same, at their life's peril, against all men and devils. This I do clearly believe to be the backbone of all Future Society, as it has been of all Past; and that without it, there is no Society possible in the world. And what a business *this* will be, before it end in some degree of victory again, and whether the time for shouts of triumph and tremendous cheers upon it is yet come, or not yet by a great way, I perceive too well! A business to make us all very serious indeed. A business not to be accomplished but by noble manhood, and devout all-daring, all-enduring loyalty to Heaven, such as fatally *sleeps* at present,—such as is not *dead* at present either, unless the gods have doomed this world of theirs to die! A business which long centuries of faithful travail and heroic agony, on the part of all the noble that are born to us, will not end; and which to us, of this 'tremendous-cheering' century, it were blessedness very great to see successfully begun. Begun, tried by all manner of methods, if there is one wise Statesman or man left among us, it verily must be;—begun, successfully or unsuccessfully, we do hope to see it!

In all European countries, especially in England, one class of Captains and commanders of men, recognisable as the beginning of a new real and not imaginary 'Aristocracy,' has already in some measure developed itself: the Captains of Industry;—happily the class who above all, or at least first of all, are wanted in this time. In the doing of material work, we have already men among us that can command bodies of men. And surely, on the other hand, there is no lack of men needing to be commanded: the sad class of brother men whom we had to describe as 'Hodge's emancipated horses,' reduced to roving famine,—this too has in all countries developed itself; and, in fatal geometrical progression, is ever more developing itself, with a rapidity which alarms every one. On this ground, if not on all manner of other grounds, it may be truly said, the 'Organisation of Labour' (*not* organisable by the mad methods tried hitherto) is the universal vital Problem of the world.

To bring these hordes of outcast captainless soldiers under due captaincy? This is really the question of questions; on the answer to which turns, among other things, the fate of all Governments, constitutional and other,—the possibility of their continuing to exist, or the impossibility. Captainless, uncommanded, these wretched outcast 'soldiers,' since they cannot starve, must needs become banditti, street-barricaders,—destroyers of every Government that *cannot* put them under captains, and send them upon enterprises, and in short render life human to them. Our English plan of Poor Laws, which we once piqued ourselves upon as sovereign, is evidently fast breaking down. Ireland, now admitted into the Idle Workhouse, is rapidly bursting it in pieces. That never was a 'human' destiny for any honest son of Adam; nowhere but in England could it have lasted at all; and now, with Ireland sharer in it, and the fulness of time come, it is as good as ended. Alas, yes. Here in Connemara, your crazy Ship of the State, otherwise dreadfully rotten in many of its timbers I believe, has sprung a leak: spite of all hands at the pump, the water is rising; the Ship, I perceive, will founder if you cannot stop this leak!

To bring these Captainless under due captaincy? The anxious thoughts of all men that do think are turned upon that question; and their efforts, though as yet blindly, and to no purpose, under the multifarious impediments and obscurations, all point thitherward. Isolated men, and their vague efforts, cannot do it. Government everywhere is called upon,—in England as loudly as elsewhere,—to give the initiative. A new strange task of these new epochs; which no Government, never so 'constitutional,' can escape from undertaking. For it is vitally necessary to the existence of Society itself; it must be undertaken, and succeeded

in too, or worse will follow,—and, as we already see
in Irish Connaught and some other places, will follow
soon. To whatever thing still calls itself by the name
of Government, were it never so constitutional and
impeded by official impossibilities, all men will natu-
rally look for help, and direction what to do, in this
extremity. If help or direction is not given; if the
thing called Government merely drift and tumble to
and fro, nowhither, on the popular vortexes, like some
carcass of a drowned ass, constitutionally put 'at the
top of affairs,'—popular indignation will infallibly
accumulate upon it; one day, the popular lightning,
descending forked and horrible from the black air,
will annihilate said supreme carcass, and smite *it*
home to its native ooze again!—Your Lordship, this
is too true, though irreverently spoken: indeed one
knows not how to speak of it; and to me it is infinitely
sad and miserable, spoken or not!—Unless perhaps
the Voluntary Principle will still help us through?
Perhaps this Irish leak, in such a rotten distressed
condition of the Ship, with all the crew so anxious
about it, will be kind enough to stop of itself?—

Dismiss that hope, your Lordship! Let all real and
imaginary Governors of England, at the pass we have
arrived at, dismiss forever that fallacious fatal solace
to their donothingism: of itself, too clearly, the leak
will never stop; by human skill and energy it must be
stopped, or there is nothing but the sea-bottom for
us all! A Chief Governor of England really ought to
recognise his situation; to discern that, doing nothing,
and merely drifting to and fro, in however constitutional a manner, he is a squanderer of precious
moments, moments that perhaps are priceless; a

truly alarming Chief Governor. Surely, to a Chief
Governor of England, worthy of that high name,—
surely to him, as to every living man, in every conceivable situation short of the Kingdom of the Dead,
—there is *something* possible; some plan of action
other than that of standing mildly, with crossed arms,
till he and we—sink? Complex as his situation is, he,
of all Governors now extant among these distracted
Nations, has, as I compute, by far the greatest pos-
sibilities. The Captains, actual or potential are there,
and the million Captainless; and such resources for
bringing them together as no other has. To these outcast soldiers of his, unregimented roving banditti for
the present, or unworking workhouse prisoners who
are almost uglier than banditti; to these floods of Irish
Beggars, Able-bodied Paupers, and nomadic Lackalls,
now stagnating or roaming everywhere, drowning the
face of the world (too truly) into an untenantable
swamp and Stygian quagmire, has the Chief Governor
of this country no word whatever to say? Nothing
but "Rate in aid," "Time will mend it," "Necessary
business of the Session;" and "After me the Deluge?"
A Chief Governor that can front his Irish difficulty,
and steadily contemplate the horoscope of Irish and
British Pauperism, and whitherward it is leading him
and us, in this humour, must be a—What shall we
call such a Chief Governor? Alas, in spite of old use
and wont,—little other than a tolerated Solecism,
growing daily more intolerable! He decidedly ought
to have some word to say on this matter,—to be in-
cessantly occupied in getting something which he
could practically say!—Perhaps to the following, or
a much finer effect?

Speech of the British Prime Minister to the floods of Irish and other Beggars, the able-bodied Lackalls, nomadic or stationary, and the general assembly, outdoor and indoor, of the Pauper Populations of these Realms.

"Vagrant Lackalls, foolish most of you, criminal many of you, miserable all; the sight of you fills me with astonishment and despair. What to do with you I know not; long have I been meditating, and it is hard to tell. Here are some three millions of you, as I count: so many of you fallen sheer over into the abysses of open Beggary; and, fearful to think, every new unit that falls is *loading* so much more the chain that drags the others over. On the edge of the precipice hang uncounted millions; increasing, I am told, at the rate of 1200 a-day. They hang there on the giddy edge, poor souls, cramping themselves down, holding on with all their strength; but falling, falling one after another; and the chain is getting *heavy*, so that ever more fall; and who at last will stand! What to do with you? The question, What to do with you? especially since the potato died, is like to break my heart!

"One thing, after much meditating, I have at last discovered, and now know for some time back: That you cannot be left to roam abroad in this unguided manner, stumbling over the precipices, and loading ever heavier the fatal *chain* upon those who might be able to stand; that this of locking you up in temporary Idle Workhouses, when you stumble, and subsisting you on Indian meal, till you can sally forth again on fresh roamings, and fresh stumblings, and ultimate descent to the devil;—that this is *not* the plan; and

that it never was, or could out of England have been
supposed to be, much as I have prided myself upon it!

"Vagrant Lackalls, I at last perceive, all this that
has been sung and spoken, for a long while, about
enfranchisement, emancipation, freedom, suffrage,
civil and religious liberty over the world, is little other
than sad temporary jargon, brought upon us by a
stern necessity,—but now ordered by a sterner to
take itself away again a little. Sad temporary jargon,
I say; made up of sense and nonsense,—sense in small
quantities, and nonsense in very large;—and, if taken
for the whole or permanent truth of human things, it
is no better than fatal infinite nonsense eternally *un-
true*. All men, I think, will soon have to quit this, to
consider this as a thing pretty well achieved; and to
look out towards another thing much more needing
achievement at the time that now is.

"All men will have to quit it, I believe. But to you,
my indigent friends, the time for quitting it has palpably arrived! To talk of glorious self-government,
of suffrages and hustings, and the fight of freedom
and suchlike, is a vain thing in your case. By all
human definitions and conceptions of the said fight
of freedom, you for your part have lost it, and can
fight no more. Glorious self-government is a glory
not for you,—not for Hodge's emancipated horses,
nor you. No; I say, No. You, for your part, have
tried it, and *failed*. Left to walk your own road, the
will-o'-wisps beguiled you, your short sight could not
descry the pitfalls; the deadly tumult and press has
whirled you hither and thither, regardless of your
struggles and your shrieks; and here at last you lie;
fallen flat into the ditch, drowning there and dying,

unless the others that are still standing please to pick you up. The others that still stand have their own difficulties, I can tell you!—But you, by imperfect energy and redundant appetite, by doing too little work and drinking too much beer, you (I bid you observe) have proved that you cannot do it! You lie there plainly in the ditch. And I am to pick you up again, on these mad terms; help you ever again, as with our best heart's blood, to do what, once for all, the gods have made impossible? To load the fatal *chain* with your perpetual staggerings and sprawlings; and ever again load it, till we all lie sprawling? My indigent incompetent friends, I will not! Know that, whoever may be 'sons of freedom,' you for your part are not and cannot be such. Not 'free' you, I think, whoever may be free. You palpably are fallen captive,—*caitiff*, as they once named it:—you do, silently but eloquently, demand, in the name of mercy itself, that some genuine command be taken of you.

"Yes, my indigent incompetent friends; some genuine practical command. Such,—if I rightly interpret those mad Chartisms, Repeal Agitations, Red Republics, and other delirious inarticulate howlings and bellowings which all the populations of the world now utter, evidently cries of pain on their and your part,—is the demand which you, Captives, make of all men that are not Captive, but are still Free. Free men,—alas, had you ever any notion who the free men were, who the not-free, the incapable of freedom! The free men, if you could have understood it, they are the wise men; the patient, self-denying, valiant; the Nobles of the World; who can discern the Law of this Universe, what it is, and piously *obey* it: these, in late sad times, having cast you loose, you are fallen captive to greedy sons of profit-and-loss; to bad and ever to worse; and at length to Beer and the Devil. Algiers, Brazil or Dahomey hold nothing in them so authentically *slave* as you are, my indigent incompetent friends!

"Good Heavens, and I have to raise some eight or nine millions annually, six for England itself, and to wreck the morals of my working population beyond all money's worth, to keep the life from going out of *you*: a small service to you, as I many times bitterly repeat! Alas, yes; before High Heaven I must declare it such. I think the old Spartans, who would have killed you instead, had shewn more 'humanity,' more of manhood, than I thus do! More humanity, I say, more of *man*hood, and of sense for what the dignity of man demands imperatively of you and of me and of us all. We call it charity, beneficence, and other fine names, this brutish Workhouse Scheme of ours; and it is but sluggish heartlessness, and insincerity, and cowardly lowness of soul. Not 'humanity' or manhood, I think; perhaps *ape*hood rather,—paltry imitancy, from the teeth outward, of what our heart never felt nor *our* understanding ever saw; dim indolent adherence to extraneous hearsays and extinct traditions: traditions now really about extinct; not living now to almost any of us, and still haunting with their spectralities and gibbering *ghosts* (in a truly baleful manner) almost all of us! Making this our struggling 'Twelfth Hour of the Night' inexpressibly hideous!—

"But as for you, my indigent incompetent friends, I have to repeat with sorrow, but with perfect clear-

ness, what is plainly undeniable, and is even clamorous
to get itself admitted, that you are of the nature of
slaves,—or if you prefer the word, of *nomadic, and
now even vagrant and vagabond, servants that can find
no master on those terms;* which seems to me a much
uglier word. Emancipation? You have been 'emancipated' with a vengeance! Foolish souls, I say the
whole world cannot emancipate you. Fealty to ignorant Unruliness, to gluttonous sluggish Improvidence,
to the Beerpot and the Devil, who is there that can
emancipate a man in that predicament? Not a whole
Reform Bill, a whole French Revolution executed for
his behoof alone: nothing but God the Maker can
emancipate him, by making him anew.

"To forward which glorious consummation, will it
not be well, O indigent friends, that you, fallen flat
there, shall henceforth learn to take advice of others
as to the methods of standing? Plainly I let you
know, and all the world and the worlds know, that I
for my part mean it so. Not as glorious unfortunate
sons of freedom, but as recognised captives, as unfortunate fallen brothers requiring that I should command you, and if need were, control and compel you,
can there henceforth be a relation between us. Ask
me not for Indian meal; you shall be compelled to
earn it first; know that on other terms I will not give
you any. Before Heaven and Earth, and God the
Maker of us all, I declare it is a scandal to see *such*
a life kept in you, by the sweat and heart's-blood of
your brothers; and that, if we cannot mend it, death
were preferable! Go to, we must get out of this un-
utterable coil of nonsenses, constitutional, philan-
thropical &c., in which (surely without mutual hatred,

if with less of 'love' than is supposed) we are all
strangling one another! Your want of wants, I say,
is that you be *commanded* in this world, not being able
to command yourselves. Know therefore that it shall
be so with you. Nomadism, I give you notice, has
ended; needful permanency, soldier-like obedience,
and the opportunity and the necessity of hard steady
labour for your living, have begun. Know that the
Idle Workhouse is shut against you henceforth; you
cannot enter there at will, nor leave at will;—you
shall enter a quite other Refuge, under conditions
strict as soldiering, and not leave till I have done with
you. He that prefers the glorious (or perhaps even
the rebellious *in*glorious) 'career of freedom,' let him
prove that he can travel there, and be the master of
himself; and right good speed to him. He who has
proved that he cannot travel there or be the master
of himself,—let him, in the name of all the gods,
become a servant, and accept the just rules of servitude!

"Arise, enlist in my Irish, my Scotch and English
'Regiments of the New Era,'—which I have been
concocting, day and night, during these three Grouse-
seasons (taking earnest incessant counsel, with all
manner of Industrial Notabilities and men of insight,
on the matter), and have now brought to a kind of
preparation for incipiency, thank Heaven! Enlist
there, ye poor wandering banditti; obey, work, suffer,
abstain, as all of us have had to do: so shall you be
useful in God's creation, so shall you be helped to
gain a manful living for yourselves; not otherwise than
so. Industrial Regiments"—[*Here numerous persons,
with big wigs many of them, and austere aspect, whom
I take to be Professors of the Dismal Science, start up*

in an agitated vehement manner; but the Premier reso-
lutely beckons them down again]—"Regiments not to
fight the French or others, who are peaceable enough
towards us; but to fight the Bogs and Wildernesses
at home and abroad, and to chain the Devils of the
Pit which are walking too openly among us.

"Work, for you? Work, surely, is not quite undiscoverable in an Earth so wide as ours, if we will
take the right methods for it! Indigent friends, we
will adopt this new relation (which is *old* as the
world); this will lead us towards such. Rigorous conditions, not to be violated on either side, lie in this
relation; conditions planted there by God Himself;
which woe will betide us if we do not discover, gradually more and more discover, and conform to! Industrial Colonels, Workmasters, Taskmasters, Life-
commanders, equitable as Rhadamanthus and inflexible
as he: such, I perceive, you do need; and such, you
being once put under law as soldiers are, will be discoverable for you. I perceive, with boundless alarm,
that I shall have to set about discovering such,—I,
since I am at the top of affairs, with all men looking
to me. Alas, it is my new task in this New Era; and
God knows I too, little other than a redtape Talking-
machine and unhappy Bag of Parliamentary Eloquence
hitherto, am far behind with it! But street-barricades
rise everywhere: the hour of Fate has come. In
Connemara there has sprung a leak, since the potato
died; Connaught, if it were not for Treasury-grants
and rates-in-aid, would have to recur to Cannibalism
even now, and Human Society would cease to pre-
tend that it existed there. Done this thing must be.
Alas, I perceive that if I cannot do it, then surely I

4—3

shall die, and perhaps shall not have Christian burial!
But I already raise near upon Ten Millions for feed-
ing you in idleness, my nomadic friends; work, under
due regulations, I really might try to get of"—[*Here
arises indescribable uproar, no longer repressible, from
all manner of Economists, Emancipationists, Constitu-
tionalists, and miscellaneous Professors of the Dismal
Science, pretty numerously scattered about; and cries of
"Private Enterprise," "Rights of Capital," "Voluntary
Principle," "Doctrines of the British Constitution,"
swollen by the general assenting hum of all the world,
quite drown the Chief Minister for a while. He, with
invincible resolution, persists; obtains hearing again:*]

"Respectable Professors of the Dismal Science, soft
you a little! Alas, I know what you would say. For
my sins, I have read much in those inimitable volumes
of yours,—really I should think, some barrowfuls of
them in my time,—and, in these last forty years of
theory and practice, have pretty well seized what of
Divine Message you were sent with to me. Perhaps
as small a message, give me leave to say, as ever there
was such a noise made about before. Trust me, I have
not forgotten it, shall never forget it. Those Laws of
the Shop-till are indisputable to me; and practically
useful in certain departments of the Universe, as the
multiplication-table itself. Once I even tried to sail
through the Immensities with them, and to front the
big coming Eternities with them; but I found it would
not do. As the Supreme Rule of Statesmanship, or
Government of Men,—since this Universe is not
wholly a Shop,—no. You rejoice in my improved
tariffs, free-trade movements, and the like, on every
hand; for which be thankful, and even sing litanies if

you choose. But here at last, in the Idle-Workhouse movement,—unexampled yet on Earth or in the waters under the Earth,—I am fairly brought to a stand; and have had to make reflections, of the most alarming, and indeed awful, and as it were religious nature! Professors of the Dismal Science, I perceive that the length of your tether is now pretty well run; and that I must request you to talk a little lower in future. By the side of the shop-till,—see, your small 'Law of God' is hung up, along with the multiplica-tion-table itself. But beyond and above the shop-till, allow me to say, you shall as good as hold your peace. Respectable Professors, I perceive it is not now the Gigantic Hucksters, but it is the Immortal Gods, yes they, in their terror and their beauty, in their wrath and their beneficence, that are coming into play in the affairs of this world! Soft you a little. Do not you interrupt me, but try to understand and help me!—

—"Work, was I saying? My indigent unguided friends, I should think some work might be discover-able for you. Enlist, stand drill; become, from a nomadic Banditti of Idleness, Soldiers of Industry! I will lead you to the Irish Bogs, to the vacant deso-lations of Connaught now falling into Cannibalism; to mis-tilled Connaught, to ditto Munster, Leinster, Ulster, I will lead you: to the English fox-covers, furze-grown Commons, New Forests, Salisbury Plains: likewise to the Scotch Hill-sides, and bare rushy slopes, which as yet feed only sheep,—moist up-lands, thousands of square miles in extent, which are destined yet to grow green crops, and fresh butter and milk and beef without limit (wherein no 'Foreigner can compete with us'), were the Glasgow sewers once opened on them, and you with your Colonels carried thither. In the Three Kingdoms, or in the Forty Colonies, depend upon it, you shall be led to your work!

"To each of you I will then say: Here is work for you; strike into it with manlike, soldierlike obedience and heartiness, according to the methods here prescribed,—wages follow for you without difficulty; all manner of just remuneration, and at length emancipation itself follows. Refuse to strike into it; shirk the heavy labour, disobey the rules,—I will admonish and endeavour to incite you; if in vain, I will flog you; if still in vain, I will at last shoot you,—and make God's Earth, and the forlorn-hope in God's Battle, free of you. Understand it, I advise you! The Organisation of Labour" — — [*Left speaking*, says our reporter.]

'Left speaking:' alas, that he should have to 'speak' so much! There are things that should be done, not spoken; that till the doing of them is begun, cannot well be spoken. He may have to 'speak' seven years yet, before a spade be struck into the Bog of Allen; and then perhaps it will be too late!—

You perceive, my friends, we have actually got into the 'New Era' there has been such prophesying of: here we all are, arrived at last;—and it is by no means the land flowing with milk and honey we were led to expect! Very much the reverse. A terrible *new* country this: no neighbours in it yet, that I can see, but irrational flabby monsters (philanthropic and other) of the giant species; hyænas, laughing hyænas, predatory wolves; probably *devils*, blue (or perhaps blue-and-yellow) devils, as St Guthlac found in Croyland long ago. A huge untrodden haggard country, the 'chaotic battle-field of Frost and Fire;' a country of savage glaciers, granite-mountains, of foul jungles, unhewed forests, quaking bogs;—which we shall have our own ados to make arable and habitable, I think! We must stick by it, however;—of all enterprises the impossiblest is that of getting out of *it*, and shifting into another. To work, then, one and all; hands to work!

CAMBRIDGE
PLAIN TEXTS

COMPLETE LIST

Each volume consists of 50–80
by a short biographical

BOUND IN

English

BACON. The Advancement of Learning. Book I.
BYRON. The Vision of Judgment.
CARLYLE. The Present Time.
DONNE. Sermons XV and LXVI.
FULLER. The Holy State (II, 1–15).
GOLDSMITH. The Good-Natur'd Man.
GOWER. Selections from *Confessio Amantis*.
HENRYSON. The Testament of Cresseid.
HOOKER. Preface to *The Laws of Ecclesiastical Polity*.
JOHNSON. Papers from *The Idler*.
JONSON. The Sad Shepherd.
MONTAIGNE. Five Essays, translated by John Florio.
SPENSER. The Shepheards Calender.

French

BOSSUET. Oraisons Funèbres.
DE MUSSET. Carmosine.
DESCARTES. Discours de la Méthode.
DIDEROT. Paradoxe sur le Comédien.
DUMAS. Histoire de mes Bêtes.
GAUTIER. Ménagerie Intime.
HUGO, VICTOR. Eviradnus *and* Ratbert (*La Légende des Siècles*).
LA BRUYÈRE. Les Caractères, ou les Mœurs de ce Siècle.
LAMARTINE. Méditations.
MICHELET. Saint-Louis.
MOLIÈRE. L'Amour Médecin *and* Le Sicilien.
MOLIÈRE. La Critique de l'École des Femmes *and* L'Impromptu de Versailles.
MONTALEMBERT. De l'Avenir Politique de l'Angleterre.
PASCAL. Lettres Écrites à un Provincial.
RONSARD. L'Art Poétique *and* Cinq Préfaces.

small octavo pages of text, preceded

note on the author

LIMP CLOTH

German

GRILLPARZER. Der Arme Spielmann *and* Erinnerungen an
Beethoven.
HERDER. Kleinere Aufsätze I.
HOFFMANN. Der Kampf der Sänger.
LESSING. Hamburgische Dramaturgie I.
LESSING. Hamburgische Dramaturgie II.

Italian

ALFIERI. La Virtù Sconosciuta.
GOZZI, GASPARO. La Gazzetta Veneta.
LEOPARDI. Pensieri.
MAZZINI. Fede e Avvenire.
ROSMINI. Cinque Piaghe.

Spanish

BOLÍVAR, SIMÓN. Address to the Venezuelan Congress
at Angostura, February 15, 1819.
CALDERÓN. La Cena de Baltasar.
CERVANTES. Prologues and Epilogue.
CERVANTES. Rinconete y Cortadillo.
ESPRONCEDA. El Estudiante de Salamanca.
LOPE DE VEGA. El Mejor Alcalde, el Rey.
LUIS DE LEÓN. Poesías Originales.
OLD SPANISH BALLADS.
VILLEGAS. El Abencerraje.
VILLENA: LEBRIJA: ENCINA. Selections.

SOME PRESS OPINIONS

-compliance

3LW, UK

9